SAN FRANCISCO

Merry Christmas ⟶
to Jenny.
All best,
Leah Gerchin

SAN FRANCISCO

The City's Sights and Secrets | Text by Leah Garchik

CHRONICLE BOOKS
SAN FRANCISCO

Library of Congress
Cataloging-in-Publication
Data available.

ISBN 10: 0-8118-5346-2
ISBN 13: 978-0-8118-5346-0

Manufactured in China.

Book and cover design by
John Sullivan and Dennis
Gallagher/Visual Strategies.

Photo research and photo
editing by David Hamlet/
Visual Strategies.

www.visdesign.com

Distributed in Canada by
Raincoast Books
9050 Shaughnessy Street
Vancouver, British Columbia
V6P 6E5

10 9 8 7 6 5 4 3 2 1

Chronicle Books LLC
85 Second Street
San Francisco, California
94105

www.chroniclebooks.com

Contents

INTRODUCTION

You want to be in the middle of San Francisco, feeling the fog on your face and smelling the salt air, experiencing it all at once. So, especially if you've flown into town, forget your first glimpse of the outskirts. Imagine that your eyes were closed as you came north past the first ring of hills and into the city. Open them only when you are engulfed by the city, when garlands of trim on the faces of hillside Victorians resemble festoons of frosting on layers of wedding cake, when the fronds atop tropical palm trees melt into the

summer mist, or when rays of afternoon sun bouncing off the windows of office buildings gleam like nuggets of gold, which was what the place was all about in the beginning.

The details are magical, but look beyond, to the horizon, at the setting that makes this show so special. It's likely that you'll see water in any one direction, hills in another, and perhaps a combination of water and hills in a third. On at least one horizon, light and shadow will be frolicking around some gift of the local topography. Somewhere there's likely to be a pink streak in the sky, bumping against a lingering tuft of gray morning fog or the first cloud of visible evening moisture. Walk a few blocks—and take courage; it may be an up-and-down route, with a few twists of the roadway in between—and you'll find yourself at the waterfront, where people are hiking, running, skating, surfing, sailing.

All this at the tip of a peninsula, in a city a little less than 49 miles square. It's an apt number around here, because it was the forty-niners who came to California in the gold rush and who built this place from a village into a gaudy boomtown into the radiant and sophisticated city it is today. All new San Franciscans

consider themselves heirs to that forty-niner tradition. "Open your golden gate" is in the first line of the city song's chorus; this is a place of welcome, and it's a place of treasure hunting.

But it's not exactly a melting pot, and the voices speaking many languages and expressing even more points of view remain distinct. We live together, but no one feels obliged to become remolded in some universal notion of what a San Franciscan is, or what a San Franciscan thinks. Lively argument abounds. No city project is completed without discussion, referendum, campaign, dissent, politicization, and, in many cases, polarization. Will taking down a freeway create an urban Eden? Will taking down a freeway add to traffic? Will taking down a freeway ruin local business? We argue, we vote, we sue, we argue again, we demonstrate and testify and picket and. . . .

Then we sit together in the darkened movie theater, where an organist still plays nightly, and just before the movie begins, he strikes up "San Francisco," that official song. And everyone claps and sings—whether they know the words or not, and more often the latter—and suddenly, we're all living in harmony.

The musical metaphor for San Francisco isn't one note. It's a chord, the sound of many tones together, and sometimes they seem dissonant. Still, each note enriches every sound and satisfies every sense, and the haunting melody of the city lingers even after the bleat of its foghorns has quieted.

DOWNTOWN

Most American cities' downtowns are defined by narrow concrete corridors, the shadows of buildings darkening the sidewalks. But San Francisco's Union Square, the traditional heart of the retail district, pays homage to a more ancient version of urban life, when city centers were sunlit piazzas.

The square's name derives from its use for pro-Union rallies before the Civil War. The monument in the middle was dedicated by Theodore Roosevelt in 1903. A hundred

years later, redesign created an open-air parlor, to be shared by shoppers and office workers, visitors and locals, lingering together over bag lunches and cappuccinos.

LEFT AND ABOVE

The 97-foot-tall column honors Commodore Dewey's victory in the Spanish-American War. The model for Victory, the figure at its top, was Alma de Bretteville, who later married sugar baron Adolph Spreckels. "Big Alma" Spreckels became one of the city's major patrons of the arts.

15

The Quake of '06

It was dark and still at 5:16 a.m. on April 18, 1906, and then the earth began to heave. The great earthquake lasted for 48 seconds, a shuddering eternity to terrified victims. Sleeping San Franciscans were thrown from their beds as the walls of their homes swayed, twisted, and crashed into splinters. At the eastern end of Market Street, the clock on the Ferry Building stopped dead.

The worst damage was to come. Ruptured gas lines, crossed electric wires, broken chimneys, and overturned stoves caused fires that roared through the city, as aftershocks continued to shake the ground. Broken mains left firefighters without water, and a series of explosions were set off deliberately in hopes of stopping the flames from eating the remaining buildings, most of which were built of wood.

For three days and nights, the fire raged, destroying an estimated 28,000 structures and turning the city to ashes. Although the fatality count was at first set at only 478—possibly to protect the reputations of those whose plan to thwart the fire with explosions had failed—modern historians put it at more than 3,400.

But those who survived refused to let their ambitions die in the embers. "After what we have gone through," one wrote, "nothing is too difficult for us to accomplish."

RIGHT

The arched arcade of the Federal Reserve Building, near the foot of Market Street, imparts physical grace to the setting for the serious work that goes on in the bank, which serves more than a third of the nation's landmass and is the largest of 12 Federal Reserve Banks in the country. Exhibits inside explain the nation's monetary system.

TOP

Ruth Asawa, sculptor, mother of six, and founder of a program to bring art to public schools, created the Hyatt Fountain near Union Square in 1973. The work employs bronze versions of dough, paper, and recycled materials traditionally used by school-children.

ABOVE

Embarcadero Center, conceived as a "city within a city," is a center of commerce on the site of the Barbary Coast, the city's first red-light district. The eight-acre complex includes 120 shops and restaurants and a four-screen movie house in five office towers, where 14,000 people work.

ABOVE

The domed stained-glass ceiling over the Garden Court of the Palace Hotel canopies what was the hotel's carriage entrance when it reopened in 1909. Tea in the court became a society tradition, as were dinner dances, parties, and cotillions. A dip in interest in such activities in the wild-and-woolly '60s proved to be temporary.

LEFT

In a city where restaurants provide entertainment as well as sustenance, the Tadich Grill, oldest in the state of California, stands out for honoring its roots and keeping up tradition. The fish is fresh and simple, the waiters' aprons are starched, and it's unlikely that a server will introduce himself by his first name.

LEFT

The Old Mint, on Fifth Street, built of sandstone at a cost of $2 million and dedicated in 1874, has been handed over to the San Francisco Museum & Historical Society, which will turn it into the official San Francisco Museum. The Granite Lady, as the only financial institution operating after the quake of '06, became the treasury for the city's relief fund.

LEFT

The 11-story-tall Phelan Building, at the corner of Grant and Market, was built in 1908, after the Victorian era, but its architects combined metal framing with Victorian stylistic details. Its white-marble lobby and elevator cabs have been restored.

RIGHT

Critical Mass, a ride that starts at the foot of Market Street and heads west through the city's streets on the last Friday of every month, celebrates bicycle power (and shakes its finger at environmentally damaging autos). What the *San Francisco Chronicle* called "guerrilla theater on wheels" has spread to more than 300 cities.

The San Francisco Museum of Modern Art, in the background at left, was established in 1935 as the first West Coast museum devoted to 20th-century art. The current building, designed by Swiss architect Mario Botta, houses a permanent collection of more than 22,000 exciting, innovative, and sometimes inexplicable pieces of modern art. Across Third Street, at right, is the Martin Luther King Jr. monument, second largest in the country for King. A waterfall cascades 50 feet over the face of the monument, which includes an inscription from King's 1963 "I Have a Dream" speech: "We will not be satisfied until justice rolls down like waters and righteousness like a mighty stream."

ABOVE

Before Yerba Buena Gardens opened in 1993, city planners intended to create "an environment in the form of a magnificent urban garden" in the heart of the city, as well as a showcase for ethnically diverse art. The resulting complex includes a theater, galleries, movie house, children's museum, play structures, skating rink, bowling alley, and outdoor stage.

LEFT

The Garden's Zeum, a hands-on high-tech children's museum, is near such low-tech children's entertainments as an innovative playground and traditional carousel. Many San Francisco pleasures are adult, but here's where kids may run free, physically and intellectually.

The heart of the Civic Center, facing west onto Franklin Street, is where politics and culture mingle. From left: the War Memorial Veterans Building, City Hall, and the War Memorial Opera House. Elsewhere in the complex are the Bill Graham Auditorium, the Brooks Hall exhibition center, the Louise M. Davies Symphony Hall, the Asian Art Museum, and the main branch of the San Francisco Public Library.

The cornerstone of the present City Hall, a French–Renaissance style building, was laid in 1913, seven years after the great quake destroyed the previous one. The building was the site of Marilyn Monroe and Joe DiMaggio's wedding; it was also the site of Harvey Milk's and Mayor George Moscone's assassinations. Damage done by the Loma Prieta earthquake in 1989 resulted in a $300 million restoration, including the application of $400,000 worth of gold leaf to the outside of the dome.

Philanthropist Louise M. Davies was the major donor to San Francisco's symphony concert hall, which bears her name. Before the hall opened in 1980, the San Francisco Symphony shared the Opera House, across the street, with the opera and ballet. The sleek new building made it possible for the orchestra to play year-round, its home stays interrupted only by tours. The Grammy-winning symphony is a major draw, and the hall's 2,743 seats are usually occupied.

The Asian Art Museum moved from Golden Gate Park to its present building, once the Main Library, in 2003. The renovation of the Beaux Arts building was planned by Italian architect Gae Aulenti, whose challenge was to carve out of an 85-year-old structure a modern home for treasures 6,000 years old. The largest interior space, Samsung Hall, was once the card catalog room.

THE WATERFRONT

The 1989 Loma Prieta earthquake was a disaster for San Francisco in many ways, but it provided several opportunities that turned out to be a boon. Most notable, the freeway that ran along the Embarcadero was declared unsafe and torn down, unwrapping the gift of an accessible bay waterfront at the eastern edge of the city. The walk along the bay is punctuated with historic plaques and stopping places. In the middle is the Ferry Building and its landmark clock tower at the start of Market Street. It's here that travelers from the East used to arrive on ferries they boarded after getting off cross-country trains that stopped in Oakland.

The 48-story Transamerica Pyramid, the tallest building in San Francisco, was completed in 1972, its shape conceived to minimize shadow. The unusual design was controversial at first, but its distinctive silhouette is by now so familiar that amateur architecture critics have gone on to grouse about other structures.

Construction begins in 2006 on a new two-berth cruise terminal to occupy Piers 30 to 32, south of the Ferry Building, glamorizing the waterfront and underlining its transition from working harbor to tourist mecca. The terminal will accommodate more than 100 ships a year, many more than 1,000 feet long and 10 stories high, and will be the site of restaurants and retail spaces.

The earliest ferries linked San Francisco and Oakland in 1850, and service between Sausalito and San Francisco began 18 years later. Although the building of the Golden Gate Bridge caused ridership to decline so severely that ferries between Marin County and the city stopped in 1941, they were brought back in 1970. Today, ferries ply the bay between Alameda, Oakland, Larkspur, Angel Island, Tiburon, Sausalito, and San Francisco.

ABOVE

"Cupid's Span," a 60-foot-high fiberglass and stainless steel work by Claes Oldenburg and Coosje van Bruggen, was commissioned by Don Fisher of the Gap for a narrow pedestrian park alongside the bay. The artists envisioned the work keeping in mind its environs, "the park with the bridge, the ships and sailboats passing," and particularly striving to emphasize the visual interplay between the bridge cables and the bowstring. Honeymooners find it inspiring.

RIGHT

The first civic committee to conceive of building a bridge across the bay was formed in 1872, but it took more than 60 years for the dream to come true. The Bay Bridge was completed in 1936 as a Depression-era project that created thousands of jobs. On an average day, 280,000 cars drive its 8.25-mile length, which includes two separate spans with Yerba Buena Island in the middle. The rebuilding of its easternmost section was necessitated by damage from the quake of 1989.

The eight-foot-tall statue of Mahatma Gandhi was donated to the city by the Gandhi Memorial International Foundation in 1988. Today, icon of simplicity Gandhi finds himself amid fields of flowers and bushels of vegetables in San Francisco's land of plenty, at the Ferry Plaza Farmers' Market, which was created in 2003 as a showcase for the best of local organic foodstuffs.

The Ferry Plaza Farmers' Market, outdoors on Saturdays, Tuesdays, Thursdays, and Sundays (as a garden market), brings hordes of shoppers and snackers. If it's summer, find the perfect peach; in winter, potatoes come in a Van Gogh–worthy palette of colors. Inside stalls feature baked goods, wine, cheese, and other regional products.

The Embarcadero Freeway

The Embarcadero Freeway once made attractions along the northern edge of the city—Fisherman's Wharf, Telegraph Hill, Chinatown—directly accessible to motorists coming from the South and East Bay. Convenient though it was, it shadowed the piers and blocked the waterfront, creating a dark no-man's land under the roadway and cutting off waterfront access for pedestrians. The Loma Prieta earthquake of 1989 and resulting freeway disasters on the Bay Bridge and in Oakland convinced engineers and city planners that the structure was unsafe.

The city was in an uproar as proponents of rebuilding argued with proponents of removing. Chinatown merchants closed their stores to demonstrate at City Hall when the Board of Supervisors debated the issue. After the vote was cast, the sound of jackhammers and wrecking equipment thundered for months, huge chunks of concrete crashing down to the pavement like glaciers melting into a sea. And the neighborhood was reborn. As for the lost freeway between geographical areas, the creation of a public transit line in its path reforged the link.

28

The six-mile-long F-line begins at Castro Street and runs northeast along Market Street, making a right-angle turn to the northwest at Ferry Plaza, to run along the edge of the waterfront to Pier 39 and other tourist attractions. This open-top car is from Blackpool, England, and was built in 1934. The fleet, restored and maintained by the non-profit Market Street Railway company, includes historic street cars from around the United States, Europe, and South America.

In the late '70s, in an area that had been dominated by industrial warehouses, landscape architect Lawrence Halprin created a verdant glen for Levi's Plaza, world headquarters for the blue jeans company. Halprin's use of natural elements—blocks of granite, for instance—created serene "rural" getaways for working people on coffee breaks, "hardworking, anti-elitist surroundings for ordinary people to enjoy themselves while experiencing higher values," said the *San Francisco Chronicle*'s architecture critic, Allan Temko.

All along the bay waterfront, signs, inlaid sidewalk plaques, and art—metal pylons 14 feet tall, by designer Michael Manwaring, among them—serve as written reminders of the nautical, social, and environmental history of the harbor. They describe the lives of immigrant workers, sailors, and rough-and-tumble fortune hunters who settled the city.

Six "view podiums" along the waterfront employ old photographs to evoke the history of the site. The story told by each is relevant to the view from the place where the reader encounters the podium. Pedestrians strolling the shoreline get a view of the city from its perimeter, but also from its past.

Residents of houseboats moored at China Basin, an inlet off the bay, once lived in low-key solitude. But with the SBC ballpark next door and the nearby thoroughfare Third Street in the midst of a renaissance, the neighborhood has acquired the panache of a midcity hideaway.

LEFT

A bit farther south along Third Street, Dogpatch was an industrial area until artists discovered it. Nowadays, streetcars connecting it to downtown promise to boost the infusion of hip culture—for example, Sunday afternoon jazz jams at the Dogpatch Saloon.

SBC Park, home of the San Francisco Giants, is accessible, user-friendly, cozy, sunny, and, with a seating capacity of 41,503, almost always packed to the rafters. Constructed after years of voter debate about land use, it became the first privately financed stadium built since Dodger Stadium. Fans escaping office jobs for a summer afternoon at the ballpark have no doubt, especially if the Giants win, that the decision to build was a good one.

ABOVE

The commonly called Third Street Bridge is formally named after Lefty O'Doul, a native San Franciscan whose career as a Giants slugger began in 1928. O'Doul retired from major league baseball after only 6½ years, but went on to run a popular downtown hofbrau, where, in perfect homage, a multitude of TVs show a multitude of baseball games all season long.

LEFT

The main entrance to the ballpark, at Third and King Streets, is Willie Mays Plaza, its central point a statue of the "Say Hey Kid." Mays played 21 seasons, moving with the Giants from New York to San Francisco in 1958, and retiring with a lifetime batting average of .302. In the years when Mays played, the Giants always led the National League in road attendance.

33

LEFT

McLaren Park, on 317 acres in the southern part of the city, was a portion of a rancho granted in 1840 when California was part of Mexico. It remained uncultivated because it was so hilly. The reservoir provides irrigation for the park and a place for off-leash dogs, a rare spot in San Francisco.

LEFT

Two weekends a year, artists all across the city open their studios to browsers, including more than 250 who work at the old Hunters Point Shipyard. The "Point" community works in what was a booming shipyard/ military station, where the navy once employed 8,500 workers.

RIGHT

Mission Bay encompasses a 43-acre University of California at San Francisco research campus in the midst of a 303-acre "life science community" along Third Street just across China Basin from SBC Park. In October 1999, when ground was broken, proponents described it as the largest urban revitalization project in the history of the city. The campus will house educational programs integrating physical, mathematical, and engineering sciences, as well as research facilities for neuroscience, developmental biology, and genetics. The surrounding area will include a community center, a library, a child care center, and landscaped open space.

FISHERMAN'S WHARF

Italians who had come to San Francisco in the mid-19th century but failed to strike it rich in the gold rush were the first non–Native Americans to fish the bay. Fifty years later, they established Fisherman's Wharf at the foot of Taylor Street, where they could hawk their catches at retail stands.

This was a notion considered quaint even then, and tourists started to join the shoppers. Slowly, the purveyors of prepared food eclipsed the vendors of fresh fish, and the wharf became one of San Francisco's most readily identifiable tourist attractions.

The area is a kind of gateway to tourist-friendly attractions, including Alcatraz, cable cars, and the shops of Ghirardelli Square and the Cannery. Depending on your point of view, that makes it crowded (grumpy residents always mention the difficulty of parking) or brimming with international visitors and overflowing with inexpensive souvenir possibilities.

RIGHT

Although many of the descendants of the first Italian American fishermen have become vendors rather than hunter-gatherers, fishing boats still set out from the wharf every morning. At sea, the world of wax museums and plastic bric-a-brac is left behind. The story of man and fish is ancient, and the most beautiful sights at the wharf are still the traditional boats.

Pier 39 was conceived as a modern Fisherman's Wharf, its exterior made from lumber recycled from a 1905 pier. The complex includes a 300-berth marina, a waterfront park, an arcade, gift shops, and almost 'round-the-clock shows by street performers. Some restaurants, moved from other locations, relocated with original decor intact.

The little cable car souvenirs may come from China, but the seagulls' screams are authentic, the smell of sea is natural, and the fish is what the place is all about. Vendors offer Dungeness crab, trapped just outside the Golden Gate, king and silver salmon, sea bass, cod, sand dabs, sole, mackerel, perch, halibut, abalone, and sole.

LEFT

The walk between Fisherman's Wharf and Pier 39 is well traveled for tourists, many of whom take nearby ferries to Alcatraz or Angel Island or attractions in Marin County. The middle of the day is usually sunny, but if you plan to be there in the morning or at night, don't forget a sweater. Summer days often turn into winter nights, and sellers of sweatshirts do their best business in July and August.

RIGHT

A community of California sea lions settled in at K-dock off Pier 39 in January 1990, a few months after the Loma Prieta earthquake, a dozen years after the pier had opened. Although they seem oblivious to the hundreds of tourists who crowd together on nearby docks and snap their pictures, they've become a major attraction. Scientists say the animals enjoy each other's companionship and like the chance to rest. The same may be said of most of the tourists.

ABOVE

Sand castles are a tradition at Aquatic Park, the efforts of amateur builders garnering admiration and advice from passing visitors. In the fall at Ocean Beach, an annual building contest raises money for arts programs in public schools. Castles are created by architects and designers (who favor innovative concepts) working with kids (who favor comic book and car-crash motifs).

RIGHT

San Francisco Maritime National Historical Park includes the Hyde Street Pier, a former ferry port where landmark ships are berthed, a visitor center, a maritime museum, and a library. Among the ships at the pier are the square rigger *Balclutha*, steam ferryboat *Eureka*, and paddlewheel tug *Eppleton Hall*.

ABOVE

The USS *Pampanito*, a World War II museum memorial and National Historic Landmark berthed at Pier 45, was featured in the movie *Down Periscope*.

LEFT

The schooner *C. A. Thayer*, launched in 1895, was part of the Pacific Coast fleet that carried lumber to San Francisco from Oregon, Washington, and the forests of northern California. It was the last wind-powered commercial ship in use on the West Coast when it was retired in 1950.

Crissy Field, a former
military airport, has
been transformed into
a bird-filled lagoon
and marsh, one of San
Franciscans' favorite
strolling areas.

LEFT

The Municipal Pier
at Aquatic Park is
accessible by public
transportation, and
most of its fishermen
aren't amateurs with
sporting equipment
ordered from catalogs.
Many are unimpressed
by the view. They
are immigrants who
grew up in cultures
where dinner was their
do-it-yourself catch
of the day.

Ghirardelli Square, on the site of Domenico Ghirardelli's 1852 chocolate shop, is a complex of restaurants and shops. Its neighbor to the north is the National Maritime Museum, behind which arcs the municipal pier at Aquatic Park. The wooded hill to the left of the pier is the site of the Fort Mason Officers' Club, just across the road from the headquarters of the Golden Gate National Recreational Area.

ALCATRAZ

A *lcatraz* means "pelican" in Spanish, but the reference to the bird, one of nature's soaring and diving free spirits, has nothing to do with the chief reputation of the 12-acre fortress, as a prison. Among the most famous residents of the federal bed-and-breakfast, built in 1907, were Al Capone, Machine Gun Kelly, and Robert "Birdman" Stroud.

Although the island is best known as a place that people were desperate to escape, traffic today is hottest in the other direction. More than a million people visit every year, and tickets for the boat to the island are among the most sought-after of any tourist attraction in town.

Its original lighthouse, lit by fuel lamp and the first on the West Coast, was built in 1884. Today, the piercing beam of its rotating electrified lamp can be seen from most anywhere in the northern section of the city, even on nights when the fog is so thick that the next block is invisible.

RIGHT

Alcatraz served as a federal penitentiary for only 29 years, during which there were 14 unsuccessful escape attempts. The distance between the island and downtown San Francisco is only 1.25 miles, but the waters are choppy.

CABLE CARS

Romanticized today, cable cars are the workhorses that allowed San Francisco to grow. They were introduced in the city in 1876, invented by wire rope manufacturer Andrew Hallidie, who theorized that a car could be dragged uphill by hitching it to a cable running steadily underground.

In 1889, sixteen years after the introduction of the system, Rudyard Kipling visited from India. "They take no count of rise or fall," he wrote of the cars. "They turn corners almost at right angles, cross other lines, and for aught I know, may run up the sides of houses."

ABOVE

The cable car gripman controls the lever by which the car grabs onto the cable, the handle that engages the wooden blocks that brake the car, and the bell that resounds all along the route of the tracks.

The Hyde Street cable car begins its climb up Russian Hill near Ghirardelli Square. The clang of the bell—a communication between the gripman and the conductor—is often accompanied by the conductor's called warning, "Hang on," as the car turns 90 degrees on the tracks. Residents whose homes are along the car routes live with the constant rumble of the cable moving under the pavement.

FOLLOWING PAGES

The California Street cable car pauses at the top of Nob Hill. The Fairmont Hotel is on the right; the exclusive Pacific Union Club is behind the car; and to the left is the majestic Grace Cathedral, an Episcopalian church. Double-ended California Street cars don't have to turn around at the end or beginning of their line.

RIGHT

A car at the top of California Street on Nob Hill, ready for its descent to the Financial district. Before the cars operated, the town's swells lived on the flats, because the arduous uphill trek made hilltop homes impossible.

ABOVE

Because the cars often serve as symbols of the city, machinery and working parts are kept polished and clean, and exteriors are kept graffiti-free. Original wood and brass interiors and fittings are maintained lovingly; the cars are as stylish as their bereted gripmen and conductors.

50

The car barn on Nob Hill, open to the public, houses winding wheels for all three of the city's lines. The cables are threaded around the wheels and move at a steady rate of 9 miles per hour.

THE CABLE CAR MUSEUM

The Cable Car Museum, in the Washington/Mason cable car barn and powerhouse, is in the center of the cable system that makes the cars go. It depicts not only the workings of the cars, but also the history of its system. A deck allows visitors to watch the engines and wheels in operation, and a viewing area shows how the cables enter the building. Also on display are three antique cable cars, the earliest from the Clay Street Hill Railroad, dating from the 1870s.

In 1947, the city closed down several car lines and considered replacing them all with motor-powered vehicles. Nothing worked as efficiently as cable cars. Today, the federal government has declared the system the only mobile landmark in the country.

The cable car system was shut down and overhauled in the early '80s. Without the bells and cables, the downtown felt eerily quiet, like a house with the family out of town. The working sound of what Tony Bennett called those "little cable cars [that] climb halfway to the stars" is the indigenous music of the town.

THE BRIDGES

The San Francisco–Oakland Bay Bridge, completed in 1936, is the workhorse of the spans and freeways that pour into San Francisco. The Golden Gate Bridge was completed a year later, and if they were people, the Bay Bridge would probably be jealous. It's the younger sister, the showy 4,200-foot-long Golden Gate Bridge, that gets most of the attention.

Heralded when it was built as the longest single-span bridge on the planet—a title that was long ago eclipsed—the Golden Gate is probably still the most glamorous bridge in the world. She is definitely decked out in the most visible makeup. The sweeping arches of San Francisco's most easily recognized symbol are familiar icons of a structure that has, like the city itself, survived unpredictable seismic instability and withstood buffeting winds and traffic.

Some 800,000 admirers turned out to walk on the bridge in a 1987 celebration of its 50th birthday. The roadway flattened, but the bridge endured.

ABOVE

The top of the Golden Gate Bridge, often shrouded in fog, looms 746 feet above the water. Eleven men were killed during the building of the bridge, and the 19 men who survived after falling from the bridge into a safety net during its construction were said to be members of the Halfway-to-Hell Club.

UNDER CONSTRUCTION

The Golden Gate Bridge was built by 10 prime contractors and subcontractors, over a four-year period, at a cost (in current money) of about $1.2 billion. The bridge steel came from Bethlehem Steel plants in Pennsylvania, New Jersey, and Maryland, where it was loaded onto railcars and carried to Philadelphia. From there, it was shipped through the Panama Canal to San Francisco.

The color of most bridges is carbon black or steel gray, but the Golden Gate Bridge is International Orange, developed by engineer Joseph Strauss and consulting architect Irving Morrow. The architect believed that the color—orange vermilion in universal terminology—not only blended well with the colors of the land around the bridge, but also stood out from the sky and the sea, making it distinctly visible to ships passing under it. The theory at the time was that it fit in but at the same time stood out.

This is a philosophy echoed by the lifestyles and inhabitants of most residents of San Francisco. It's our bridge, all right.

LEFT AND ABOVE

The bridge work crew includes 17 ironworkers and 38 painters, who repair and repaint corroding steel while suspended above the water. It's not true that the bridge is being painted constantly, but other work is continually underway. There are, for example, 600,000 rivets in each of the two towers, and replacing them with bolts has been an ongoing task.

Traffic is constant, but sometimes nature takes its toll (without paying). The lowest volume of cars in the bridge's history was 3,921 southbound vehicles (about a tenth of the usual count) on January 6, 1982, after mud slides impeded the northern approaches to the bridge. The highest was after the Loma Prieta quake, which left the undamaged bridge as one of only two routes by which San Francisco drivers could circuitously reach the East Bay. On October 28, 1989, 162,414 vehicles made it across the bridge, in both directions.

LEFT AND ABOVE

Cargo ships, most bound for Oakland, enter the harbor under the Golden Gate Bridge. Meanwhile, around the footings near Fort Point on the San Francisco side, wind- and kite-surfers fearlessly ride the waves breaking against the jagged rocks that ring the shoreline. This is a dramatic site made even more so by a sense of danger, near where Jimmy Stewart pulled Kim Novak out of the water in *Vertigo*.

Sailboats and yachts are berthed at harbors just east of the Golden Gate Bridge, at South Beach, between SBC Park and the Bay Bridge, and at Pier 39. The often-frisky bay winds bring speed, and there are races on many weekends. Boats may be rented or chartered, and sailing to picnic on Angel Island is a favorite weekend activity.

Commercial vessels operating at the Port of San Francisco include tugboats, pilot boats, bar pilots, water taxis, barges, and ferries. Port authorities govern the water and the shoreline, keeping watch to make sure that all businesses occupying desirable waterfront locations have legitimate marine connections.

In 1872, Emperor Joshua Norton, a beloved civic eccentric and one of the enduring characters in local history, decreed that a bridge be built across the bay, suggesting that if the job wasn't done, city officials should be locked up. Today, local historians are proposing that the span be named after him.

A dazzling necklace of lights was first placed on the Bay Bridge in 1986 in celebration of its 50th anniversary. Residents liked the borrowed diamonds so much that drivers paying 50-cent tolls at the time voluntarily chipped in, handing toll takers dollar bills to finance making them permanent.

THE PRESIDIO

A large chunk of San Francisco, its northwest corner, has belonged to every American since 1994, when the Presidio, former headquarters of the Sixth Army, became part of the Golden Gate National Recreation Area, which stretches from south of the city to Marin County.

The 1,500-acre tract, established by the Spaniards as a fort in 1776, is thick with 60,000 trees. Structures built over the years for military purposes—offices, housing, hospitals, recreation—have been turned into headquarters for nonprofit and educational groups, the whole supported by a private-public partnership. The biggest single facility, headquarters for film-maker George Lucas's Letterman Digital Arts Center, is the enterprise that allows the Presidio to support itself. Built on the site of an old hospital and opened in 2005, the facility was designed to fit in with existing historic structures.

LEFT AND INSET

Fort Point, at the southern end of the Golden Gate Bridge, is the oldest brick fort west of the Mississippi River, built during the Civil War to protect the harbor. Adult visitors are awed by its brickwork, its interior curved stairways; children love its cannons and gun implacements.

ABOVE

On the promenade near Crissy Field, a recreational area reclaimed from military use in 2000, is the Warming Hut, a visitor center and café designed on principles of sustainability. Interior wood was salvaged, and the menu features locally produced foods.

RIGHT

George Lucas's Letterman Digital Arts Center, at the eastern edge of the Presidio on the site of a former army hospital, was landscaped by Lawrence Halprin, who designed this folly in modern homage to the traditional arched shapes of the rotunda of the nearby Palace of Fine Arts.

LEFT

In the Presidio's pet cemetery, handmade grave markers pay tribute to dogs and cats, but also to parakeets, canaries, pigeons, macaws, rabbits, hamsters, rats, lizards, and more.

East of Crissy Field, the Roman rotunda of the Palace of Fine Arts is silhouetted above a lagoon. The Palace houses the Exploratorium, a hands-on science museum that was one of the first in the world to be interactive.

The Palace of Fine Arts, designed by Bernard Maybeck for the Panama-Pacific International Exposition, has been called a "Beaux Arts hallucination." Although it was originally built as a temporary structure, its grandeur and opulence fit in so well with San Franciscans' perception of their city that it has twice been fortified and retrofitted to ensure its permanence.

THE PANAMA-PACIFIC INTERNATIONAL EXPOSITION

The Panama Canal, cause for great rejoicing in California because it cut the shipping distance between New York and San Francisco by 7,873 miles, opened in August 1914. The official civic celebration of that achievement—and the unofficial celebration of the recovery of San Francisco from its devastating earthquake of 1906—was the Panama-Pacific International Exposition, a 288-day-long party for the city.

Eight central exhibition halls, as planned by chief architect George Kelman, included homage to industrialization and homage to the arts, in the form of the Bernard Maybeck–designed Palace of Fine Arts. The building was surrounded by a Tower of Jewels, studded with bits of Bohemian glass; a Horticulture Palace; gardens landscaped by John McLaren (who had designed Golden Gate Park); a concert hall that seated 3,500; and an amusement park with carousels, dioramas, and models of parts of the Panama Canal.

The fair cost $15 million to build, and on opening day, February 20, 1915, there were 150,00 people lined up for more than a mile, all the way from Van Ness and Broadway, waiting to get in. The event was a huge success that left the city with a million-dollar surplus, enough to pay for a civic auditorium still in use.

THE QUAKE OF '89

From Bangor to San Diego, Seattle to Key West, Americans had turned on their television sets and tuned in to San Francisco. The date was October 17, 1989, and the event was the third game of the World Series, in which the San Francisco Giants were pitted against the Oakland A's. The weather was unusually still and hot at Candlestick Park, and a crowd of 60,000 fans had gathered.

At 5:04 p.m., minutes before the game was to begin, the event that had been dreaded since 1906 occurred. A major earthquake, 7.1 on the Richter scale, centered in Loma Prieta, several miles south on the San Andreas Fault, collapsed buildings, freeways, and a section of the Bay Bridge; knocked out electrical and gas lines; and caused fires and destruction.

There was no damage at all to 98 percent of the city, especially downtown, where buildings had been constructed under strict seismic regulations. But the Marina district, where most homes had been built on sand and landfill was devastated, as visible in the picture above.

Modern firefighting techniques and rescue capabilities prevented great loss of life, but power was cut off for days in some places, months in others, and most Marina residents relocated while their homes were rebuilt.

LEFT

Today, the foundations of most Marina homes having been fortified, Marina Boulevard seems both stately and Mediterranean. Fishing boats long ago disappeared, and champagne is quaffed in yacht clubs.

TOP

Peter Richards and George Gonzales's wave organ, jutting into the bay at the end of the Marina breakwater, is an environmental "instrument" that makes what has been described as the sound of "the world's largest seashell."

ABOVE

The Fort Mason Center, east of the Presidio, is home to at least 35 nonprofit arts organizations, and about 1.5 million culture lovers a year attend performances, special events, and meetings there.

There's a panoramic
view of the city from
atop Coit Tower, but
the murals inside,
painted during the
Depression by 25 WPA
artists, provide a no-
less-inspiring view,
back through time, of
the lives of working
men and women in
California. The murals
and Pioneer Park, at the
base of the tower, have
been recently restored.

Although named after
Lillie Hitchcock Coit,
a woman who loved
firefighters and who
donated the tower
in their honor, the
monument shape does
not, as early critics
said, refer to a fire
hose. The tower itself
was designed by Henry
Howard and built in
1933 by Arthur Brown,
whose other structures
include City Hall.
Howard always insisted
that the tower had no
design precedent.

NORTH BEACH

The original north shore of San Francisco disappeared when landfill created terra firma on which factories were built to provide goods for the growing town. So North Beach has no beach.

In 1890, there were 5,000 Italian Americans in the city; 50 years later, 60,000 lived in North Beach. But Chinatown was always more crowded, and when that neighborhood inevitably spilled north, the Broadway dividing line was crossed by the growing Chinese community. Nowadays in Washington Square, the scent of garlic from a foccacia bakery may waft over a t'ai chi class.

FAR RIGHT

Saints Peter and Paul Church, established in 1884 to serve the growing community of Italian immigrants, was built at its present location, dominating Washington Square, in 1924. Around its facade is verse from Dante's "Paradiso."

INSET

Chinese dance is often inspired by nature, and a traditional fan dance refers to a woman walking in a garden. Washington Square becomes that garden for regular students of outdoor fan-dance classes.

The Beat Generation

While the rest of America was turning on to rock and roll, TV sitcoms, and nuclear power, North Beach became home to the purposeful dropouts. Bohemians became Beats and iconoclasts became beatnik poets. Writers, painters, and musicians took pride in rejecting both the red-scare politics and Doris Day—in–gingham culture of the day.

Jack Kerouac's *On the Road* and Allen Ginsberg's *Howl* were read in North Beach in 1955. Poet Lawrence Ferlinghetti began his City Lights publishing company with Ginsberg's masterpiece, and was prosecuted for having published obsceni-ties. Ginsberg and Ferlinghetti were both acquit-ted, and became heroes of the Beat movement.

Although Americans in other parts of the country saw the Beats as jaded and world-weary, Ginsberg described Kerouac's philosophy as a wake-up call about "the sacredness of the world. This is the only time we're gonna be here, so it's not shit at all and it's not negligible. This is it. And if this is It, what could be more sacred? So you better appreciate it now, while it's here."

Italian North Beach coexisted with Beat North Beach, and then Chinatown seeped north of Broadway, too. Cheap apartments made it desirable. The neighborhood is hip and chic, but much of it is still working class.

Henri Lenoir was the owner of the Vesuvio, just across the alley from City Lights. The café/bar/gallery was where the first Beats congregated to drink and read poetry aloud, the first activity being a useful aid to the second.

City Lights Bookstore, founded by poet Lawrence Ferlinghetti and Peter Martin in 1953, describes itself as dedicated to carrying on "the Beats' legacy of anti-authoritarian politics and insurgent thinking."

San Francisco's Broadway entered the national consciousness most forcefully as the boulevard of girlie clubs. A sign on the Condor Club, where breast-implant pioneer Carol Doda danced topless in 1964, says it's the "Birthplace of the World's First Topless and Bottomless Entertainment." Later, testosterone still setting the scene, it became a sports bar; but finally, more generic appetites won out—it's currently a restaurant and jazz club.

The reputation of Vesuvio, a saloon just across Kerouac Alley from City Lights, as a Beat hangout was cemented in 1955, when Neal Cassady first stopped by for a poetry reading.

Although early and late fog can make outdoor dining a challenge in mid-summer, the city's strict antismoking regulations have given rise to outdoor tables, even along narrow sidewalks. A long lunch in North Beach provides the opportunity to flirt with passersby and check out the groceries toted home from the neighborhood's traditional delicatessens.

THE HILLS

Counting hillocks, slopes, plateaus, peaks, mounds, and mounts, the tally is 43 hills in San Francisco.

Twin Peaks, third highest in town, were named for their resemblance to a lady's above-the-waist assets. Other nomenclatures are similarly lofty: Nob Hill, "The Hill of Golden Promise," was once the site of the largest and gaudiest mansions in town, all but one destroyed in 1906; the name Russian Hill evokes Fabergé, but legend has it that it was the site of a cemetery for seal hunters; Pacific Heights means deep pockets, and that's why its most elegant blocks are nicknamed the "Gold Coast."

Among the others, Telegraph Hill was a communications center, Goat Hill was nanny-land, and Buena Vista and Bay View have exactly those sightlines. Corona Heights? Every hill has a distinct personality, as well as an elegant name probably bestowed by a real estate agent.

LEFT AND RIGHT

Lombard Street on Russian Hill, celebrated tourist attraction, garden spot, and, most often, site of a queue of cars waiting to descend, is not, as touted, "the crookedest street in the world," nor even in the city. That honor, geometrically calculated, goes to Vermont Street on the south flank of Potrero Hill.

The California School of Fine Arts, ancestor of the San Francisco Art Institute, moved to its Chestnut Street building in 1926. Through the court-yard, there's an open-to-the-public café with panoramic views of the bay. A Diego Rivera mural readily viewable in a gallery just past the front entrance depicts the Mexican muralist at work on a fresco, and was commissioned by the artists' school.

Tucked away between Taylor and Jones Streets on Russian Hill is Macondray Lane, a secluded tree-lined walkway on which once-modest structures—workingmen's cottages built in the 1800s, for example—have been renovated and enlarged to luxury proportions to match their real estate values. The lane, filled with ferns and shaded by tall trees and neighbor-ing apartments, is where Armistead Maupin placed his fictional *Tales of the City*.

TOP AND ABOVE

The tale of Mark Bittner befriending "the Wild Parrots of Telegraph Hill" became a book and feature documentary of the same name, with a romantic ending for the parrots and for Bittner. As to traditional romantic sites, Julius' Castle, on Montgomery Street, built in the '20s and a former speakeasy, is an ideal setting for admiring the view and one's dining companion.

RIGHT

The Filbert Steps descend from the foot of Coit Tower to the foot of Telegraph Hill, past the Art Deco house featured in the Humphrey Bogart–Lauren Bacall film noir *Dark Passage*. They are public property, but gardens alongside are painstakingly tended by individuals and neighborhood groups.

Fourth of July fireworks, set off along the northern water's edge, can sometimes be obscured by fog, but in this picture they are so bright that they seem to be coming from the roof of St. Mary's Cathedral. The church was completed in 1970, and Pope John Paul II celebrated mass there in 1987.

ABOVE

The Fountain of the Tortoise, a copy of a fountain in Rome, was on the estate of the Crocker family in Hillsborough until 1954, when it was donated to Huntington Park atop Nob Hill. The Nob Hill Association joined forces with the city's Arts Commission and the Ford Motor Company to finance its restoration in 2001.

RIGHT

The world-famous Cathedral of Chartres, France, was the inspiration for both the rose window and labyrinth at Grace Cathedral, the third largest Episcopal cathedral in the United States. Believers use the labyrinth as a meditative device, and visitors are invited to "walk it with an open mind and an open heart."

CHINATOWN

Chinese came to San Francisco as traders well before gold was discovered in California. After 1848, when news that there was gold here spread to Asia, a new wave of adventurers called Celestials set out for California, which they called the "Golden Mountain." In the 50-year period that ended at the turn of the 19th century, 320,000 Chinese settled here. In San Francisco most of the newcomers lived in Chinatown, which had been one of the city's oldest neighborhoods and became one of the world's largest settlements of Chinese outside Asia.

The first Chinese who arrived were allowed to rent rooms only on Stockton Street. Chinatown spread east and west from there, and started becoming a tourist attraction around 1910.

Dragon's Gate, the city's showiest entrance to Chinatown and the portal that separates it most distinctly from downtown, was donated to San Francisco by the People's Republic of China in 1969. The inscription on the gate, which is at Bush Street and Grant Avenue, translates as, "The reason to exist is to serve the public good."

San Francisco sculptor Benjamin Bufano's rendition of Sun Yat-sen, founder of the Republic of China and the Kuomintang party, is in St. Mary's Square, near Old St. Mary's Church. The Bufano work was commissioned by the WPA.

Waverly Place, once called "15 Cents Street," for the price of cutting a pigtail, is most famous for temples, among them the multistory Tien Hau. Also open for browsing is the Clarion Music Center, at the corner of Sacramento Street, which sells exotic instruments from around the globe.

ABOVE

Chinatown festivities often feature dragon and lion dances, accompanied by the popping of firecrackers and the pounding of drums. The young people who run alongside guide the beast as it moves through the streets.

MIDDLE LEFT

The Green Street Mortuary Band is hired by more than 300 grieving families a year, to ward off evil spirits by parading about 12 blocks through the streets of Chinatown and making noise as well as music. The Christian hymns, dirges, and marches of the band are purported to ward off evil spirits.

BOTTOM LEFT

Chinese herbalists claim to cure what ails you, using a variety of ingredients to banish baldness, flatulence, insomnia, impotence, and other conditions no one wants to admit having. Even if you're a perfect specimen and you're not in the market, some of the herb stores date back to the '20s, so it's worthwhile to peer in at the cabinetry.

CHINESE LABORERS AND IMMIGRANTS

Chinese who had left Asia dreaming they would find gold in California found instead, during the 1870s and 1880s, that they had been indentured to pay back the cost of their passage.

Most worked as laborers, putting in long hours for low wages, earning little but the animosity of other workers, who resented their wages being undercut.

In 1880, Congress passed the Chinese Exclusion Act, denying citizenship to Chinese immigrants. Four years later, Chinese women were banned from setting foot in the United States. Illegal female immigrants, many of them barely teenagers, were forced into lives of prostitution.

In the midst of World War II, in 1943, President Franklin Delano Roosevelt finally moved Congress to vote to repeal the Chinese Exclusion Act. But it wasn't until 1946, in the War Brides Act, that Chinese women were given permission to immigrate to the United States.

THE CHANGING CITY

Probably the most famous picture of San Francisco puts its painted ladies, pre-earthquake Victorians that survived the fire, in the foreground, its modern downtown behind. The fire of '06 stopped at Van Ness Avenue, preserving wooden houses to the west. Almost everything east of Van Ness was destroyed and later rebuilt.

The quake of 1989 was less damaging to buildings and to people, but it wreaked havoc on freeways. When they were torn down, the waterfront and Hayes Valley areas reclaimed land that had been lost to civilization while cars roared overhead.

Mid-20th-century redevelopment projects razed many Victorian treasures (to create Japantown, for instance). But most change nowadays is mindful of preserving the architectural excesses of that era, which—along with the up-and-down landscape—make the city unique.

LEFT

Steiner Street Victorians face Alamo Square, creating a most treasured image for visitors. The grassy hill of the park facing the houses is almost always dotted with camera-toting visitors.

Exterior-house-painting firms often specialize in Victorians, and many homes have plaques crediting the color schemes. Most originally were painted in neutral colors; the '70s brought a rainbow of hues to the streets.

ABOVE LEFT

The San Francisco Architectural Heritage Foundation is headquartered on Franklin Street, in the the Haas-Lilienthal House, a Queen Anne Victorian mansion constructed of redwood in 1886. The house was built for William Haas, who was born in Bavaria and came to San Francisco in 1868, when he joined a grocery firm.

ABOVE RIGHT

There are only two left of the eight octagon houses that were in San Francisco, and the one at Gough and Union contains a museum run by the National Society of Colonial Dames of America. The house was designed by a doctor concerned that residents receive sufficient sunlight.

St. Mary's Cathedral was designed by Pier Luigi Nervi, employing striking form, a crosslike hyperbolic paraboloid, and, at the entrance, his signature lacelike use of metal and stained glass.

RIGHT

The dome of Sherith Israel Synagogue is lavishly painted in lush patterns. The landmark California Street building was used as a temporary city hall after the earthquake of 1906.

LEFT

The annual Cherry Blossom Festival features a colorful parade, the sound of Taiko drummers booming through the streets, and, of course, children's and adults' community groups hawking sidewalk fusion cuisine: hot dogs and stir-fry.

THE MISSION

Mission Dolores, at the heart of San Francisco's thriving, throbbing Mission district, is an oasis of dignity, faith, and tradition. The mission itself was founded in 1776, and its building, constructed by Franciscans, was completed 15 years later. It is the oldest structure in the city.

The interior of the church features doors from the Philippines and altar parts from Mexico among the architectural elements that reflect Spain's international importance in the 18th century. Outside, some of San Francisco's earliest settlers are buried in the adjacent cemetery.

The nearby neighborhood demonstrates the strength of its Latino roots. A walk along Mission Street is a stroll through Mexico, Colombia, Guatemala, Nicaragua, and El Salvador, in the largest settlement of Central Americans outside their lands.

INSET

Mission Street is where locals shop, and Valencia Street is where they eat. Every traditional cuisine is represented (Mexican burritos, Vietnamese pho, Chinese pot stickers, Indian nan, Belgian crepes, Jewish bagels, and more), as well as mixed-up versions such as tofu burritos and jalapeño bagels.

RIGHT

Samba schools send feathered dancers through the streets at Carnaval, in late spring, and the sounds of salsa, samba, and gospel set a joyous beat. A vibrant and colorful parade of floats and dancers proceeds through the neighborhood for hours, and the whole city joins the Latino fiesta.

Food shopping in the Mission district— where the variety of chiles matches the variety of gems at Tiffany's—is distinctly different than in North Beach, Chinatown, or the Richmond district.

The purpose of the missions, to convert Native Americans to Catholicism, is reflected in the building's interior, where basket designs of the Costanoans provided the inspiration for patterns on the ceiling. During renovations in 2004, religious murals painted by indigenous people in 1791 were discovered behind an altarpiece that had blocked them from view since 1796.

Dolores Park, first inhabited by Ohlone Indians, became a Spanish rancho, then a Jewish cemetery. In 1905, the city bought the land, and a year later, it became a refugee camp for 1,600 families who had fled the fire after the earthquake.

The park is often used as a place of assembly for political demonstrators on their way to City Hall. Because of its sunny Mission district weather, it's also the stage for many outdoor concerts and performances, and the San Francisco Mime Troupe opens annual shows there every July 4.

THE CASTRO AND BEYOND

The Castro district lies at the last flat part of Market Street, before it begins climbing Twin Peaks. Until 1854, it was part of a Mexican-owned ranch; afterward, it was subdivided into parcels for what we now call blue-collar families. Today, it is the center of what's probably the most famous gay and lesbian neighborhood in the country, brimming with successful retail businesses you might find in most any community in the country. Visit on Halloween night, when costumed revelers and drag queens fill the streets, and see how it's different from most every other community in the country.

RIGHT

Castro Street is the site of a giant annual Halloween party, with a fishnet-and-feathers dress code, whatever the weather. This is an event for adult goblins, with grown-up sensibilities and many devils in the crowd.

INSET

The Charles M. Holmes Campus at the San Francisco Lesbian Gay Bisexual Transgender Center is the first in the country in a facility constructed for that purpose. It was built with more than $11 million in private donations and is used by more than 2,000 visitors every week.

LEFT

The houses of almost any city neighborhood are chronological reflections of architectural diversity. Fancy-pants Victorians and crisp stucco structures lean against each other as they march sideways up and down the hills. Although front lawns are a rarity in San Francisco, backyards are surprisingly green and tree-studded.

ABOVE

San Franciscans trying to gauge the weather habitually glance west along Market Street to Twin Peaks to see if the fog's lurking. Experienced amateur forecasters can estimate how many minutes of sunshine are left from the position of the cloud hovering around Sutro Tower, which aids TV transmission.

RIGHT

San Francisco Bay is visible in the distance from the Saturn Steps, near Roosevelt Way and 17th Street, just above the Castro district.

99

THE HAIGHT

There are more than a thousand Victorian homes in Haight-Ashbury, where in 1967 the Summer of Love blossomed. Nearby Golden Gate Park provided an outdoor venue for music, dancing, communal meals, and smoking illegal substances, until rampant drug use turned the neighborhood into a "psychedelic ghetto" for drugged-out panhandlers. Just as the area hit bottom, young people taking advantage of real estate bargains returned, and the Haight was reborn. Today, chic moms push expensive strollers past sidewalk loungers. Like geologic strata in rock formations, the residents of Haight-Ashbury clearly demonstrate their neighborhood's eccentric history.

ABOVE

The "art car" is a Haight-Ashbury tradition, with vehicles decorated in homage to motif (the sea car is covered with shells), individual (Dalí, for example), or politics (heck no to whoever got elected).

Shoppers and visitors
find themselves among
aging hippies, pros-
perous home owners,
teenage runaways, and
camera-toting tourists
looking for the ghost of
Janis Joplin. The Haight
is endlessly redefined,
but the previous era is
never quite erased.

GOLDEN GATE PARK

ost San Franciscans live in houses pressed together against the sidewalk, so they regard Golden Gate Park as the country. The park extends from the Pacific Ocean on the west to its eastern end at the Panhandle, which juts out and ends halfway through the city.

John McLaren, superintendent of the park for more than 50 years, turned natural sand dunes into a leafy planned wilderness. Leisure facilities—casting pool, lawn bowling, tennis courts, stables—are spread throughout, creating special interest areas even in this natural-feeling habitat. But McLaren liked nature more than he liked manmade things, so you'll have to look among trees to see statuary and monuments, most of which are tucked neatly into recesses.

The Japanese Tea Garden, five acres of complex plantings of both Japanese and Chinese origins, a pond, bridges, and a teahouse, was designed by Makato Hagiwara, who also invented the fortune cookie.

Would-be yachtspersons can rent rowboats, motorboats, or pedal-powered boats at Stowe Lake, where the waterway is shared with ducks and turtles.

ABOVE AND LEFT

The de Young museum, one of the two art institutions that make up the Fine Arts Museums of San Francisco, reopened in 2005 in a striking copper-clad building and tower by the Swiss architects Herzog & de Meuron. British artist Andy Goldsworthy's "Drawn Stone," at the entrance to the museum, is a site-specific work in which a crack that runs jaggedly through pavers and boulder/benches reflects California's tectonic topography.

The Bay to Breakers, held every May, is a race from the eastern edge to the western edge of the city, 7.6 miles. "Race" is a fudging word, because only a few thousand runners are serious competitors. Most of the more than 100,000 people in this ritual romp are in costume, except for the couple of dozen every year who run naked.

Golden Gate Park's buffalo were introduced to the park in 1892, when they lived there alongside elk, bears, and goats. At one time, each bore the name of a Shakespearean character—picture Ophelia as a shaggy beast—but in the early 1990s, with a nod to political correctness, they were rechristened with Native American names.

LEFT

The "Dutch" windmill near the northwest corner of Golden Gate Park was built at the behest of John McLaren, who realized that sea breezes might be used to pump as many as 100,000 gallons of water an hour from underground streams and rivers to irrigate his beloved park. Around the restored mill is the Queen Wilhelmina Tulip Garden. A similar mill at the southwest corner of the park is being restored.

RIGHT

The National AIDS Memorial Grove in Golden Gate Park, maintained by volunteers, pays homage to the thousands who have died from the disease and the thousands who have cared for them. The idea for the Grove was established in 1989, and its development, on a 7.5-acre dell in the park, was begun two years later. Engraved into the flagstone floor of the Circle of Friends, one of its most-visited sections, are the names of more than a thousand people, living and not, whose lives have been impacted by AIDS.

THE AVENUES

A long the northern and southern borders of Golden Gate Park, extending toward the ocean, are the Richmond and Sunset districts, with avenues numbered into the 40s. "The Avenues" is the familiar local term for these neighborhoods. (Ironically, the broader numbered roadways downtown are called "Streets"; Fifth Street is decidedly wider than Fifth Avenue.)

Looking at the structures in the Richmond and the Sunset, one would think the mix of people who live there is fairly homogenous. The neighborhoods contain block upon block of one- or two-flat houses built after the '20s, on land that was once dunes. But the city's complex history of immigration waves is reflected in individual neighborhood pockets. The selection of groceries in corner stores tells more about the ethnic mix than a map.

INSET

Russian immigrants have come to San Francisco since its earliest days, but the biggest wave arrived as refugees from communism in the '80s. They jumped into capitalism enthusiastically, well-stocking Richmond district delicatessens with smoked fish, sausage, and homemade pickles.

RIGHT

Many blocks of side-by-side houses in the Sunset district were built in the late '40s and early '50s, for the families of veterans returning from World War II. The neighborhood, bordered in the west by the Pacific Ocean, was called the "Outside Lands."

The Ingleside Terraces
Sundial, near the intersec-
tion of Ocean Avenue and
Junipero Serra Boulevard,
on the site of a racetrack
that had closed in 1905,
was dedicated in 1913.
With a 34-foot clock face
diameter, it was said to be
the world's biggest sundial.
Dedication ceremonies
were held on the day that
the Atlantic and Pacific
Oceans were to meet to
form the Panama Canal, a
year before that waterway
was completed.

ABOVE

Grand View Park's northerly view is of the
Sunset district, Golden Gate Park, and then the
Richmond district and the Golden Gate Bridge. It
is reserved for special occasions, when the fog is
polite enough to remain over the ocean.

RIGHT

Four cemeteries
once took up all
of the Richmond
district. But when
the city's growing
population made
land scarce, a
1901 law forbade
city burials; most
graves were moved
to the suburb of
Colma. Remaining
on Lorraine Court,
near Arguello
Street, is the
Columbarium,
built in 1897 as a
repository for ashes
and mementos of
the departed.

LANDS END

I t was Alma de Bretteville Spreckels, the woman who posed for the top of the Union Square monument, who gave the city its grand Palace of the Legion of Honor. Her mother had worked as a laundress, but Alma was a descendant of a French general, and she was a devoted Francophile.

After she married sugar baron Adolph Spreckels, the couple traveled to France, and she convinced him to finance a museum that would focus on French art. The city donated the land, a gloriously well-situated hilltop parcel between Sea Cliff and Land's End. Alma Spreckels insisted the museum be modeled on the 150-year-old Palais de la Legion d'Honneur in Paris.

It opened on Armistice Day in 1924, and was dedicated to 3,600 California soldiers killed in France during the Great War. The Legion houses print and porcelain collections, but its focus is ancient and European art.

INSET

The golf course at Lincoln Park was built on the grounds of a former cemetery in 1908. It is the site of the annual San Francisco City Golf Championship, the oldest continuous golf event in the United States.

LEFT

Mark Di Suvero's 1999 "Pax Jerusalem" stands near several monuments linked to the Legion's international focus. A cast of "The Thinker" in the museum's central courtyard is 1 of 70 artworks donated to the museum by its original benefactor, Alma Spreckels.

The Cliff House

When the Cliff House was built in 1863, it was accessible only by private carriage traveling from downtown on a toll road. Two years later, the Great Highway was completed, and local swells began arriving in numbers. And when Belgian-born engineer, inventor, millionaire (and eventually mayor) Adolph Sutro bought the Cliff House and built a railroad to provide public transportation to weekend revelers, it became accessible to all. By the turn of the century, on a weekend day, 1,200 carriages would vie for parking spaces (a San Francisco tradition).

Scenic though it was, the site seemed cursed. A schooner crashed into the foundations of the Cliff House in 1887, and a following explosion demolished a large section of the building. On Christmas Day 1894, it burned to the ground. Two years later, Sutro spent $5,000 to build a seven-story-tall Cliff House, styled like a French chateau, with a 200-foot-tall observation tower. That one, pictured above, went up in smoke in 1907.

After that fire, wary sea lions abandoned Seal Rock for the Farallon Islands, more than 20 miles out to sea. It wasn't until 1909, when Sutro's daughter opened a third Cliff House to the public, that they returned, apparently as curious and eager to see the place as tourists who make it a regular stop. The Sutros sold the building in 1952.

Just north of the Cliff House, only ruins remain of the Sutro Baths, a public swimming establishment built in 1896 at a cost of $1 million. Patrons swam laps of luxury in seven heated pools, some with saltwater, some with man-made waves, and there were trapezes, slides, and high-diving areas. The whole structure was destroyed by fire in 1960. Locals with childhood memories of the place tell tales of mandatory woolen bathing suits that sagged when wet.

The Cliff House was acquired by the National Park Service in 1977 and is part of the Golden Gate National Recreation Area. It was renovated in 2005, and contains a formal restaurant, café, bar, and party facilities.

The Beach Chalet, designed by Willis Polk, opened in 1925 with a lounge, a restaurant, and changing rooms for beachgoers. In 1936, Lucien Labault painted WPA-sponsored murals of scenes of San Francisco in the Depression. Luckily, these survived the era when the Chalet was closed to the public and used as barracks for military troops. A visitors' center focuses on Golden Gate Park lore, and the Chalet has restaurants upstairs and down, the lower a glass-ceilinged open-air dining room.

RIGHT

A hang glider leaps from the cliff at Fort Funston, catching a current of wind, soaring along the shoreline, and hovering over the surf. The hills around the fort contain dismantled artillery turrets and pillboxes that were built to guard the coast during World War II. Today the area, windblown and rough, is the Champs-Elysées of dog walkers.

BELOW

The San Francisco Zoo, which focuses on conservation, contains a three-acre African savanna inhabited together by giraffes, zebras, kudus, ostriches, and other forms of wildlife. The Primate Discovery Center provides plenty of space for at least five endangered species of monkeys and their relatives to climb and swing, while human primates discover the length of their children's attention span.

ABOVE

The annual summer festival at Stern Grove makes all kinds of musical performances—symphony, opera, ballet, world music—available to the picnicking public free. The recently renovated Grove, situated in a natural amphitheater, features comfortable lawn spaces for blankets, but bring sweaters to ward off the fog, which seems to like the music, too.

FACING PAGE

The waves look gentle at Baker Beach, but a strong undertow and ferocious currents make the water unsafe for swimming. Nonetheless, children and dogs often frolic nearby. The northern end is a nude beach, not quite right for those children but fine for the dogs, who don't seem to pay close attention.

ABOVE

A fisherman tries his luck in the fog at Baker Beach, just west of the Golden Gate Bridge. The scene is timeless, except for his cigarette. When the day heats up, the fog burns off, and walkers hit the beach for daily constitutionals, he'll probably get some guff about that. For the moment, however, this is San Francisco, a place where the cover of fog makes everything possible.

Photo Credits

AKIM AGINSKY

akim@aginsky.com
www.fifthframe.com

Photos © 2006 by Akim Aginsky on pages 58, 106 bottom left

ROSLYN BANISH

roslynbanish@sbcglobal.net

Photos © 2006 by Roslyn Banish on pages 19 bottom left, 26 top left, 30 top, 42 top, 65 top, 67 bottom, 68-69 center, 74 right, 88 right, 90, 91 top, 99 bottom, 102-103 left, 105 top, 105 bottom center, 107, 110-111 right, 116-117 right, 119

MARK BITTNER

www.wildparrotsbook.com
www.wildparrotsfilm.com

Photo © 2006 by Mark Bittner on page 79 top left

RICHARD BLAIR

rk@richardblair.com
www.richardblair.com
www.pointreyesvisions.com

Photos © 2006 by Richard Blair on pages 17 top right, 25 right, 26 right, 40 left, 41 left, 42 bottom, 50 right, 52-53 left, 54-55 left, 55 center, 56, 59, 73 bottom left, 100 left, 103 right, 104 bottom, 106 top left, 118

MIKE BLUMENSAADT

mike@matrixphotographics.com
www.matrixphotographics.com

Photos © 2006 by Mike Blumensaadt on pages 11 top left, 14-15 left, 15 right, 21 top, 21 bottom, 25 left, 27 right, 28-29 center, 29 right, 30 bottom, 33 left, 110 top left, 114 right, 116 left, 116 bottom

FRANCIS DESILVA

www.photovault.com

Photo © 2006 by Francis DeSilva/ Photovault on page 81 left

HANK DONAT

Photos © 2006 by Hank Donat on page 19 right

PAUL GRADY

Photo © 2006 by Paul Grady on page 73 top

BILL GOIDELL

www.photovault.com

Photos © 2006 by Bill Goidell/ Photovault on pages 10 left, 22 bottom, 83 right

BILL HANNAPPLE

williamhannapple@hotmail.net

Photos © 2006 Bill Hannapple on pages 20, 39 bottom, 41 right, 44-45 right, 68 top left, 81 right, 115 top

DENNIS HEARNE

sunnyco@earthlink.net
www.sunnyco.net

Photos © 2006 by Dennis Hearne on pages 2-3, 18-19 left, 31 top, 35, 38 left, 39 top, 69 bottom, 71 left, 72 left, 74 left, 74-75 right, 85 center, 86-87 left, 92 center, 95, 99 top, 108 center, 108-109 right, 110 bottom

DON KELLOGG

kelloggphoto@yahoo.com
www.kelloggphoto.com

Photos © 2006 by Don Kellogg on pages 4-5, 9, 17 bottom left, 46 right, 50 left, 51 left, 60, 61, 85 top left, front cover

BRUCE KLIEWE

Photo © 2006 by Bruce Kliewe/ Jeroboam on pages 76-77 left

WERNHER KRUTEIN

admin@photovault.com
www.photovault.com

Photos © 2006 by Wernher Krutein/ Photovault on pages 16 right, 17 top left, 17 bottom right, 19 top left, 22 top, 23 bottom, 32, 33 right, 34 top, 37, 62-63 left, 63 center, 64, 70 right, 71 right, 73 bottom right, 78 left, 78 right, 79 bottom left, 84, 88 left, 89, 91 bottom, 96 left, 98, 100-101 center, 104 top, 112-113 left, 113 right, 115 bottom

FRED LINDEN

Photos © 2006 by Fred Linden on page 57 bottom

GREGG MANCUSO

Photos © 2006 by Gregg Mancuso/ Jeroboam on pages 23 top, 43, 47

JUNE A. OSTERBERG

jaosterberg@earthlink.net

Photo © 2006 by June A. Osterberg on page 28 top left

KENT RENO

Photos © 2006 by Kent Reno/ Jeroboam on pages 38 right, 44 left

SUSAN SCHWARTZENBERG

www.exploratorium.edu

Photo © 2006 Exploratorium on page 69 top

JAMES C. SULLIVAN

Photo © 2006 by James C. Sullivan on page 11 bottom right

JOHN SULLIVAN

Photos © 2006 by John Sullivan on pages 31 bottom, 34 bottom

TOM TRACY

Photos © 2006 by Tom Tracy on pages 1, 8, 12-13, 24, 46 left, 70 left, 77 right, back cover

SEAN VALLELY

hadleysean@earthlink.net
www.bluefortyseven.com

Photos © 2006 by Sean Vallely on pages 6-7, 48-49, 53 right, 57 top, 79 right, 80, 92-93 right, 96-97 right

NANCY WARNER

Photos © 2006 by Nancy Warner on pages 82-83 left, 85 bottom

DAVID WEINTRAUB

dweintraub@bellsouth.net
www.weintraubphoto.com

Photos © 2006 by David Weintraub on pages 27 left, 36 left, 40 right, 65 bottom, 66, 94 right, 94 left, 106 right

We are grateful to the San Francisco History Center of the San Francisco Public Library for providing the historical photos which appear on pages 16 top left, 51 right, 55 top right, 67 top right, 72 top right, 85 top right, 114 top left.

Photo on page 16 top left from the Collection of Roy D. Graves, Courtesy of The Bancroft Library, University of California, Berkeley.